Colossi

Colossi

Poems by

David Capps

Cover design by Shay Culligan

ISBN: 978-1-952326-43-1

Kelsay Books
502 South 1040 East, A-119
American Fork, Utah, 84003

Acknowledgments

Many thanks to the various journals that have published my work over the last few years:

Peacock Journal: "Colossi," "Some Remarks on the Poetry of Rain," "Prayer (moon)," "Field Mice Speak"

Mantra Review: "A Mycology after Christopher Smart"

Anima: "Prayer (sea)"

Isacoustic: "Orestes," "Atrium," "Breezes," "Denoument"

Portrait of New England: "Meditation at Sleeping Giant, Hamden, CT"

Spiritus: "An Attempt to Imagine the Origin of Christianity from Another World"

Plainsongs: "Appassionata"

"Voúves II" and "I could ask the shepherd for you" were published by Yavanika Press as part of my chapbook, *A Non-Grecian Non-Urn.*

Contents

Desert Landscape

I reflect in the canyon
on the canyon I reflect

in. I appear present in
such natural light,

the nature of which is:
Ideas of soul shrink

from view, enveloped
by red sand (life is

there, too). Aloneness,
loathsomeness rest,

become cicadas buried
in dark. This is what

light comes to when
it fills the canyon: non-

distinction. The sound
of helicopters flying

over the silent opening
of cactus flower.

"I could ask the shepherd for you"

Morning's blue-grey light appears
from the veranda (I have just stepped out, continuously
unable to sleep

Overlooking the Ikarian sea, an urgelessness, diaphanous
blue (I loom to cast it as a spell, to settle it compactly
as the scent

of dittany and sea salt.
Inside, bundles of sage hang from the rafters,
as if they were barnacles

on a lost ship. As if I could walk into my all of dreams
toward the tincture
of goat bells in the hills,

never mind what it means to express
the populous sums of my saturnine rings falling away
from weariness.

Prayer (sea)

that they move with a sea
the color of soapsuds,
rosemary as paper,
water as stone,
an iridescent
whole,
souls
so
full of prayer in the rush to tell them
selves the impossible—

yet no one
in this plenum, where the slightest dew mirrors
a kiss of infinitely smaller
machines
can ask for this—Curious thing,
the sea of heads rising, crests of faces falling
who ask for what is necessary
and reveal it in that
asking

as if an ear holding the weight of that sea
could hear across the widest shore—

so the eye pauses as silent lightning
falls   wants now to take you in its arms
to tell you…

Breezes

Breezes die
like persuasion:

buds opening
and closing

with waning
sunlight,

a monk's
bowl, filled

with petals
or rice,

what we find
difficult

in time's keep.

On the Very Idea of a Problem: A Poem for the Anthropocene

In the dream the problem was he couldn't see a smile
as continuous with a face.
In most dreams we see clocks without faces, or hands

discontiguous with clock faces. In most realities
I don't see this *as* a problem. Yet in most problems
the feeling of reality is faceless.

I suppose that the most pressing problems
we fail to see at all. They arise, dissipate, ice clouds in mimosas,
so completely as fresh cut grass

staring back at us greenly. Whose smile enshrouds
the countless similitudes. What then feeling is it, is it
being in love? Is death even *like* it?

Gratuitous slippers. The purple of evening's calm
descent. The measureless mountains in reversal. Wind-scrawl
across grass in a storm.

You as a human as an individual as a woman as a writer as a lover
as a violinist as a daughter or son as someone's
hover there while

a gift of owls green as night climbs your open eyes, climbs
the railing of your eyes
to see you for the first time

as the Earth's.

Strategic Foresight

Unlike your offshore rig, the slump of land
is fragile, and its source the earth
is fragile, and the surveyor walking, at his own slant
is fragile, but who really cares?

He's almost marching, fat and with spittle
sounds, spittle sounds and the footfalls
of a bumpkin lawyer—less versed, I'm sure,
in the moral law, if it exists.

His face turns to a launch of sparrows
outside range of hills, dogs, clods of clay—
What would it mean for our words
to alight with such purity, like a butterfly skimming

a water drop? What would it mean for you,
if no one were looking, following, leading up
to some proposition like "we dig here"?
                              Something unsayable buds

below the significance of any proposition,
a thing that just isn't "is, is, is", or the *heres*
and *theres* of shovel stumps, or an elevated
standing reserve.

Shredded roots of maples hold to the wet
pulse of the ground rending—rendering
what is Caesars unto Caesar—
in short, everything, as you play at stewardship

of Earth, and water
is as oil filling up the lungs of songbirds
painlessly.

Colossi

Chemiburnt and tundried excrescence through hall blakoncrete hyperwalls gearing staged neon glass loudspeaks initial III companichols screenoil rean threadbare multiwoodbetween filaments conferencing satisfaction drilling probing blind teleprompters metallic noise soldering public architectural works squandering corrosive bolts of greasebank blue hooked in march of blank facesconveyors of black shoes

until a storm breaks open arc welders thunder lift their masks a window verdanterre as childhood

peasantly logjam day's aloed aherd whence golden colonies encircle sinless sun yellow hinds in wickened air wheat colored drapery of ice and honey—

Switches behind, we clambered   towards white rocks
                                      bodies shining
                                        chisel
                                        donkeys scraped
                                        hawed on the cliff,
                                        chewing sage and thyme
                                        all birds of the sea rose to
                                        meet us
                                        on bank of salt and beak

    we whirl-pooled
                              to the bubbling corpus
                              of the mountain that had starved
                              its dry grit unchanged by wind
                              where Colossi like tusks
                              jutted out from its navel
                              mythically as wings
                              of monarchs
                              resolving into stars.

Field Mice Speak

Of stars as emptied out of a vase
in patterns of tough equations.

Small questions arise about
drinking flower-heads: who

put them there and why? Some
of the light, as if fallen into

a hex, bends with the squint
of an eye. What shall we name

her, this mouthless glass-blower
who stands by the banks

of overpowering wheatgrass?

Prayer (moon)

The moon outside my bedroom window,
same moon by whose light a child holds
his hands together and whispers, moon

shining above the desert waste, where
snakes wait curled in rock crevices,
same moon that unites different worlds,

a candle that clears away the darkness
and allows us to see spirit undestroyed,
and body lifted as into your blue cradle.

Remind us once again of the importance
of sadness.

Spring Digression

began I with a framework
for analyzing Spring—its greens and grueish brooks
      that time when in the dark I wondered about the black swan
          of its projectible predicate
             and felt that I was either green before you
died or blue afterwards, spells of selfless little words like streams
dreamt my very eyes
a fat witch chanted
threatened to pass out on my pathetic love seat
      a black swan proved grues to be incoherent
          errands went by the by in such dank depressions as
could be found

in the spiraling stacks where gunrunners who'd walked so far in
Madagascar
gave up, knees just as swollen as monks
      quickly I was becoming one of the order, wasn't I kneeling
          on each step, my pale eye….

in my own mind during this time I had not yet mastered a public
language, so?
if I really needed to I could back up, to when I ran
      with the wind, "at One," my backyard a funnel web, the
currents
      as currents imagined from some tidal drill

then I was the perspective of the butterfly's perspective landing on
my finger
amid aerial assaults of leaves and cotton wisps
      we surfaced as lightly, like sailboats skimming earth's outer
layer
      and sweet earth allowing it

haven't you ever wondered why it is that in the blue light
        before dawn
your body appears so soft that its contours
        seem like the nexus of hands and fruits
                seem almost to dissolve beneath the gaze as the
mouth

as though gaze and mouth which had been so incommensurable
before
were rendered the same
        as though senses were one organ made manifest
                in this unique condition—so the land has lost itself in
darkness

before dawn you have lost yourself, uncovered, simultaneous
sensuous failures
to distinguish yourself from yourother

        and consciousness a clock whose second hand someone
presses
                gently down and pauses

whose time you pause within can never be your own, and you recoil
in shock
at this or something quite like this…

A Mycology after Christopher Smart

Because we ourselves exist in that region between plant and animal
liminal with transcendent selves
Because we would love to be caressed outward from our center
flesh, nervous system permitting
Because each rainfall holds up a mirror from which our children
spring, as in May, gleeful with laughter
Because any dried leaf could be from Eve, who fell with the rain
like it even mattered to the colors' contrast
Because you are so resistant to Fall
Because flushing, or sweating, or saying thanks, is one spore print,
and being kind is another
and none of these are marks of the mind
Because at the base of a stump made to hug the earth and beside it
an unidentifiable red worm crawls
Because I am always there with you although you never know
where I'll be
Because when a puffball suspends its microscopic wings a hush of
vernal perfume runs over you
Because a pitch soil a swamp soil an abandoned bark barely
enough to keep afloat, does not deter you
Because our surfaces can never be cleansed that they must be taken
as they are
Because the appearance of solidity can draw you to your roots
Because when I draw you it is constantly childish and comical
everything I am not
Because unlike a man who has been destroyed you can be returned
to glory, even after a long bath in the sun
Because we peek from under the covers at what lies ahead while
you sit openly in the remains of the day
Because between the bottom of the well and the sky a meadow is
strewn with you

Because you go unnoticed
Because for you there are no more hiding places in the soft spots
of the clouds
Because we must become creatures with time-anguished eyes

Shade

Love meets love not yet born
in the shade of the fig tree

grown up against the gate
in the middle of the blue field.

The soft belly of a Jacob's sheep
rises and falls beside the tree,

a rhythm established in time.
Whoever you are falls silent.

Grant me this one thing: that I
may embrace you as my eyes

cleave to the whole of winter
wheat.

That Part of You

                                   starclusters   neighbors
                                   glad to see you   to finally meet
                                   the indestructible you   that part of
you

blossoming out in spiraling arms to go on and on
that indefinite walk with you
you walk indefinitely

                                   and you go   smiling less
                                   the lotus eaters' milky invitations to tease
you flutter far afield

you go

Über Alles

Rain falls, striations
of glass. After a paper
cut, it rains courage,

or not quite courage,
but a spreading-over
all, über alles.

A child buries his head
in a shoulder. His father,
though ash, is still

the Black Forest. He is
a tree the axe skipped
in the density

of wilderness. That is,
before he grew old
and hollow. Years before

they made him part desk
and part floor.

Meditation at Sleeping Giant, Hamden, CT

Still myself among
tall pines,

my mind rises
as a mist

in morning. Clear
motes fall,

mute needles
glissando

along an endless
fingerboard,

carillon bells
call gospel

songs, sonorous
in depth,

as if they had
avowed

to disinherit
the earth.

Mind is
a crystal glass,

tipped on end,
ringing,

even before
the touch.

Practicing Paganini

          He leans, locked   chinrest, yet
free   ,   free will is free,
                 hovering ~~over~~ desire's   , its split
quadruplestops,   sharpshooters

                      that   debate
       self and non-~~self~~, blameless
          movement   salmon,   glinting   air
upstream   seldom
             real tears, bow-taut, expressive,
                 way up the body's
          bow

               such dexterity
          up the fingerboard of their lives,
        eyes, fingers, *about* nothing,

=

          How I was sure   the fish was a bird
How sure   of the fish   bird
          How sure I was the fish was a bird
How sure
          How sure I was that   life came back
in my hands   for instance

          is spring

Appassionata

A bird alight a phoenix stone. Iterations
of words. Allegro assai across a headstone,
faded squall of tail feather, forefinger trilling
white keys, an appassionata sonata. Wants

the stone sculpture to be a fountain, wants
to be a bird, to have a small reflection cross
the water, a warmth to erupt through snow.
Lines inscribed on gravestones, emboldened

by her small clawing, her miscellaneous
fluttering which makes certain names appear
and reappear. Bird in greek was palm for phoenix,
phoenix in greek was palm for bird, palm

in greek, phoenix for bird, phrases scratch away,
phrases in phrasis, atavisms on brownstone,
atoms in tightly packed stone planes, molecular
condensations, condescensions, engines of false

spring, as if so much had gone into my attempt
to make sense of it, but not enough.

Inscription

Morning comes   the blue eye
as in the path of thirty-five or so headstones,

brownstone-carved angels celebrating its light
by standing so

completely still   the names, sibylline
in their sleeping letters,

as lips closed while sleeping, become visible.
Then work:

sprinklers, dutiful, play jump rope on the grass
already soft with dew,

the blue eye blots out the shape of the sun,
sensuously tracing "O"

O the groundskeeper trims back long hedges
of his recurring dream

until there are none.

Some Remarks on the Poetry of Rain

I

The rain's falling is poetic if only because it emphasizes
the spaces between things.

Listening to the rain helps one learn to see.

II

Imagining the rain, imagining listening to the rain,
do not really differ. One never hears a first drop fall,
one always notices that *it has begun* to rain.

III

Raining is like the waters breathing,
in shining droplets
the waters seeing.

IV

Rain trickles down, solitary conversants
in an unknown language, while from time to time
a bemused ethnographer looks up:

How would I know before my thoughts are expressed
in this language, that they do not first occur
in the language of the rain?

V

Dogen said: Decheng guiding his disciple is his disciple.
Perhaps the rain guiding my language
is my language.

Denouement

When it was over, I looked
over the sea (the sun half-

full) of prepositions: *of*
and *for* rose amid waves,

seemed shadows shorn *from*
sleeping elbows I knew,

a light-dark light-dark *to* I
looked forward to.

Atrium

At dusk we ate salad:
green leaves enfolded their lives
for us, curled on the tines

of a fork. A cricket you thought
was the ship's engine sang
beneath your chair.

The song I couldn't guess
rehearsed in the hull's massive iron
head, a language to itself.

Evening after evening, the weeks
unbuttoning blue blouses
vanished over sea rifts. Wakes

the ship left of pure white clouds
collided unabridged.
There was peace.

Accession along the Neckar River, Tübingen

Willow branches in the slow-flowing Neckar, a mute swan's
vestibule.
She slips through green reeds

a wake of gondolas trails behind her, the watery folds of her dress
vanishing in golden light.

Plane trees shine into evening. Broad leaves rehearse their lines,
each poised on a semi-translucent lip,

as if sentiment had grown its memento mori. Such regalia as a leaf
pivoting on its narrow axis,

blighted axis in the water's hollow, drop away as I walk forward
beneath the moon.

An Attempt to Imagine the Origin of Christianity from Another World

(for Simone Weil)

I

Juniper berries
rise to the lake's surface:
pale moons,

as if the Earth had many
such moons, and you were
an odd duck,

a desperate man, an oil
painter living long ago,
trying to capture

essential colors
of as many as you could.
As if you had thought:

what would revive us,
truly, is to become shadows
of ourselves, to move

at the snail's pace
of another sun, as ice
drips from juniper twigs

blue shadows
brush, eyelashes at the far end
of an otherworldly pale

blue lake.

II

But to what can we compare
at this rate, what ration
when an erosion throws it

all in: pickerel weed, sweet
flag, arrowhead—death's
grip?—A blood fugue?

Undeniably, mountain laurel
suffers. Your hands tense
around their bolt,

all the worlds in perpetual
erosion, values
of a partial function

that returns "true" only
once, skinny fingers
working a press

that can only apologize
mechanically, over and over
again. Bullet casings

with the lake's muted
sheen, falling
to the factory floor's red.

III

A sigh arises
at the sight of juniper berries
surfacing, this time

not as moons. As near-expressionless
children, and then,
from one child, merely

possible—(before you storm out,
throwing your paints and easel
against the wall),

a figure emerges.

IV

A red Christ, with
a crown of thorns, walking
across the calm,

as if impossible and possible
were the same.

V

A blue Christ, carried
beneath the constellation Virgo,
pointing toward that

by which possible and impossible
are the same.

VI

The most delicate lines you try
to connect them.

Prayer (earth)

May you hear me, this pearl reflecting your light
in rays as eyebeams and none to record how they fall,

for it is not in a straight line, but radiating from all sides,
that you shine from every corner of Being, equally,

thus may the pearl within me mirror your reflectance;
yet I, that small part of me who now *thinks* to pray,

strangled elderberry branch reaching toward the source
on this parched day, may that part ascend, changed.

Orestes

What if in years
you find yourself
flying as a bird
with one wing

falling as a note
of some far being
who is all-seeing
down to the least

crease you find—
would that be
yourself folded
into one thought

for one thought
less moment, air
you shake off
with a flaunt
of tail feather,

for what awaits?
Our wishes, or
what were ours,
are oars swept
to sea, and small

sky flecks, light
as gulls, points
of possibility,
intersecting

lines that seem
to tell you, and
speak as softly
as might, to let

that Orestes die
who hides inside
whose signs dive
so null and deep.

Upon Seeing the Ancient Olive Tree at Voúves, Crete

Of all calamities: lightning, drought, blight, wildfire
Minoan hand-axes
blazing through,

and yet

The whole green chandelier in loving
disarray, where to touch one leaf is felt throughout
the whole.

The still wind plays across
mute crystals, now one, now another, cluster
in Aeolian.

Later, ovular lights shining from the inhabited
peninsula strike us
as gently:

"hope", "time", "peace", appear and fade, a host
of associations, a king's
initials.

Voúves II

At Voúves, standing as you take the picture
I begin to have a thought,
leaning to one side as strands of ants form
a line on the bark of this oldest
olive tree in Crete. There, in my mind/brain
electrical signals surged, ion
channels opened as they have always opened
in our species, with such fury
of hunger, lust, danger, the aesthetic of wide
horizons, shade, fruit, branches
smoothed by the laying of hands over years.
                                        Olives
hung before my thought,
whatever it would have been, could arise,
olives, *eliés,* the same word
for the raised moles on arms and shoulders,
minor interruptions of the skin's
seamless unity, that largest organ we live in,
while at the center of the spiraling
branches, rounded in purgatorial frieze,
there is a hollow large enough
to lie in under the ancient canopy, to sleep.

The Smile

The cart tipped over and the beast
with its tears in the hills.

The vocabulary of monks in margins
red-breasted with curlicues.

When in a checkout line someone
yawns beneath white light   to be

elsewise conscious than thus, perhaps
as Loki, that creature transformed

into the dark and beautiful mare
luring Svadilfari into a cave.

And how should you know if you've
slipped some additional veil

between one thought and another,
one hope and another, one past

and another? *Well then, I've perfected
the smile.*

About the Author

David Capps is a philosophy professor and poet who lives in New Haven, CT. He is the author of two chapbooks: Poems from the First Voyage (The Nasiona Press, 2019), and A Non-Grecian Non-Urn (Yavanika Press, 2019).

www.ingramcontent.com/pod-product-compliance
Lightning Source LLC
Chambersburg PA
CBHW031154090426
42738CB00008B/1325